COUNTRY PROFILES
SINGAPORE

BY NICOLE E. RODRIGUEZ MATA

BELLWETHER MEDIA • MINNEAPOLIS, MN

This edition first published in 2023 by Bellwether Media, Inc.

No part of this publication may be reproduced in whole or in part without written permission of the publisher.
For information regarding permission, write to Bellwether Media, Inc., Attention: Permissions Department,
6012 Blue Circle Drive, Minnetonka, MN 55343.

Library of Congress Cataloging-in-Publication Data

Names: Rodriguez Mata, Nicole E., author.
Title: Singapore / by Nicole E. Rodriguez Mata.
Description: Minneapolis, MN : Bellwether Media, Inc., 2023. | Series: Blastoff! Discovery: Country profiles | Includes bibliographical references and index. | Audience: Ages 7-13 | Audience: Grades 4-6 | Summary: "Engaging images accompany information about Singapore. The combination of high-interest subject matter and narrative text is intended for students in grades 3 through 8"– Provided by publisher.
Identifiers: LCCN 2022016487 (print) | LCCN 2022016488 (ebook) | ISBN 9781644877494 (library binding) | ISBN 9781648347955 (ebook)
Subjects: LCSH: Singapore–Juvenile literature.
Classification: LCC DS609 .R63 2023 (print) | LCC DS609 (ebook) | DDC 959.57–dc23/eng/20220414
LC record available at https://lccn.loc.gov/2022016487
LC ebook record available at https://lccn.loc.gov/2022016488

Text copyright © 2023 by Bellwether Media, Inc. BLASTOFF! DISCOVERY and associated logos are trademarks and/or registered trademarks of Bellwether Media, Inc.

Editor: Rebecca Sabelko   Designer: Brittany McIntosh

Printed in the United States of America, North Mankato, MN.

TABLE OF CONTENTS

MAGICAL TREES OF SINGAPORE	4
LOCATION	6
LANDSCAPE AND CLIMATE	8
WILDLIFE	10
PEOPLE	12
COMMUNITIES	14
CUSTOMS	16
SCHOOL AND WORK	18
PLAY	20
FOOD	22
CELEBRATIONS	24
TIMELINE	26
SINGAPORE FACTS	28
GLOSSARY	30
TO LEARN MORE	31
INDEX	32

MAGICAL TREES OF SINGAPORE

A family begins their Singapore vacation at the Supertree **Observatory**! They explore a vertical garden full of steel structures that look like trees. Each of the 18 trees rises up to 164 feet (50 meters) tall. Over 100,000 different plants grow on these supertrees!

4

At night, the garden becomes a magical place. Colorful lights shine from the supertrees as music plays during the Garden Rhapsody show. The family heads to the top of the tallest supertree. They look in wonder over Marina Bay and the sparkling city. This is Singapore!

LOCATION

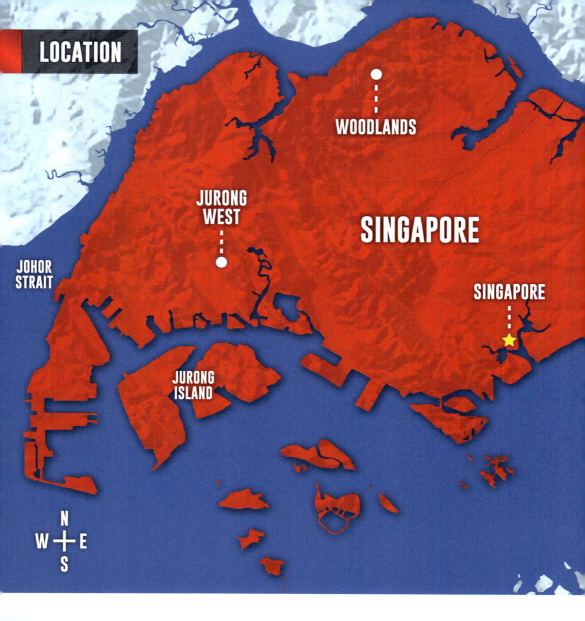

Singapore is an island **city-state**. It is located in Southeast Asia at the end of the Malay **Peninsula**. Singapore's 278 square miles (719 square kilometers) consist of the main island and more than 60 other islands. Jurong Island is the largest. It lies southwest of the main island. On the southern shore of the main island is the capital city of Singapore.

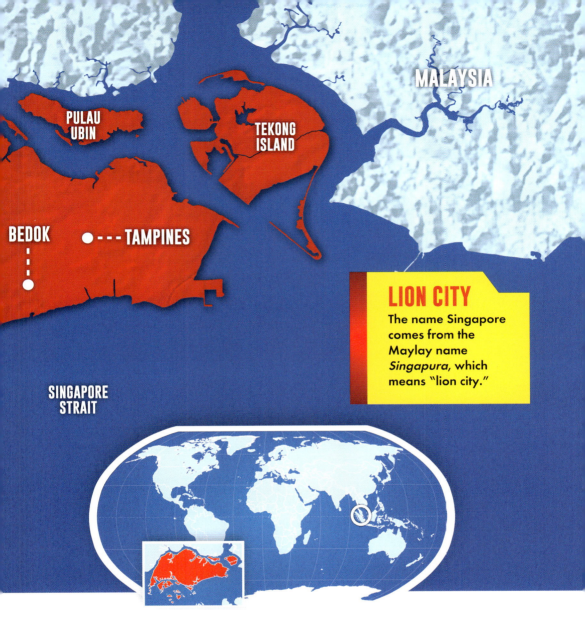

LION CITY
The name Singapore comes from the Maylay name *Singapura*, which means "lion city."

Malaysia is Singapore's closest land neighbor. They are separated by the Johor **Strait** along Singapore's northern and eastern edges. Indonesia lies to the south across the Singapore Strait.

7

LANDSCAPE AND CLIMATE

Singapore is mostly flat. However, the central region has a rough terrain with many hills. Timah Hill is the tallest. It stands 531 feet (162 meters) tall. The northern coastline is made up of large areas of wetlands and **mangroves**. The eastern region is a low **plateau**. Low but steep ridges cover the main island in the south and west. Singapore's longest river, the Kallang River, is only 6 miles (10 kilometers) long. It flows into Marina Bay.

MANGROVES

TIMAH HILL

SINGAPORE
Average seasonal highs and lows

JANUARY
HIGH: 88 °F (31 °C)
LOW: 75 °F (24 °C)

APRIL
HIGH: 90 °F (32 °C)
LOW: 77 °F (25 °C)

JULY
HIGH: 88 °F (31 °C)
LOW: 77 °F (25 °C)

OCTOBER
HIGH: 90 °F (32 °C)
LOW: 77 °F (25 °C)

°F = degrees Fahrenheit
°C = degrees Celsius

Singapore is hot and wet. It has two **monsoon** seasons. The northeastern monsoon runs from November to March. The southwestern monsoon lasts from May to September. Singapore's dry season lasts from February to April.

9

WILDLIFE

Although highly **urban**, Singapore has a lot of wildlife. In the many forest parks, Sunda flying lemurs glide between trees. They share the treetops with langurs. These shy monkeys like their homes to be quiet. Hornbills fly over the treetops. These big-beaked birds make loud calls.

Wild boars and their young search for food on the forest floor. In the rivers, families of otters playfully splash in the water. Kingfishers perch along the banks. They watch for small fish to swim by. Dolphins swim and jump in the sea waters south of Singapore.

ORIENTAL PIED-HORNBILL

WILD BOAR

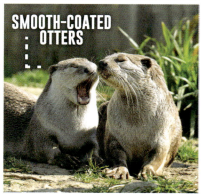

SMOOTH-COATED OTTERS

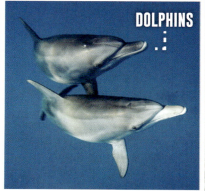

DOLPHINS

COMMON KINGFISHER

SUNDA FLYING LEMUR

SUNDA FLYING LEMUR

Life Span: unknown in the wild
Red List Status: least concern

Sunda flying lemur range = ▮

| LEAST CONCERN | NEAR THREATENED | VULNERABLE | ENDANGERED | CRITICALLY ENDANGERED | EXTINCT IN THE WILD | EXTINCT |

PEOPLE

Almost 6 million Singaporeans call the nation's islands home. Nearly three out of every four people are Chinese. Smaller populations of many other **ethnic** groups live in Singapore, too. People from Malaysia and India make up the next-largest groups.

There are four official languages in Singapore. They include English, Mandarin Chinese, Malay, and Tamil. Other Chinese **dialects** are also spoken. English is the most common language used. Many Singaporeans practice Buddhism. Christianity and Islam are also common. One in five Singaporeans do not practice any religion.

FAMOUS FACE
Name: Fann Wong
Birthday: January 27, 1971
Hometown: Singapore
Famous for: The first Singaporean woman actor in a Hollywood film, she is most known for her role in the movie *Shanghai Knights*

SPEAK MANDARIN
Mandarin uses characters instead of letters. However, Mandarin words can be written with the English alphabet so you can read them.

ENGLISH	MANDARIN	HOW TO SAY IT
hello	ni hao	nee HAOW
goodbye	zai jian	tsai JYEN
please	qing	ching
thank you	xie xie	SHYEH shyeh
yes	shi	shih
no	bu	booh

13

COMMUNITIES

CONNECTING THE ISLAND

Singapore is connected to Malaysia by two bridges. One bridge supports vehicles and trains!

Singapore is completely urban. Most people live in high-rise buildings close to parks and **nature reserves**. Smaller numbers of Singaporeans live in stilt houses along the coast. Singapore has a great public transportation system. A lot of people also get around by riding bicycles or taking water taxis.

In Singapore, family is very important. Most families are small, with a father, a mother, and one or two children. Some families have multiple generations living in one house. Grandparents often help take care of young children.

CUSTOMS

Many Singaporeans value **face** and how they are viewed in their communities. Chinese communities show respect to elderly members. They are often called "Auntie" or "Uncle," even if they are not related. In Malay and Indian communities, people wash their feet before entering **mosques** or temples.

MOSQUE

MIND YOUR MANNERS

In Singapore, it is polite to use both hands to give things like money or gifts to others.

Singaporeans like a clean city. There are many rules to follow so the city stays tidy. People are fined if they break any rules. Littering is not allowed. Eating and drinking can only be done in certain areas. Everyone does their part to keep Singapore clean and beautiful!

17

SCHOOL AND WORK

In Singapore, primary school lasts six years. Secondary school lasts four to six years. It is flexible for most students due to a track system. There are three tracks including an express track, an academic track, and a technical track. Each track can lead to either university studies or trade studies.

Almost three in four people have **service jobs**. They work as engineers, IT staff, teachers, sales representatives, or financial analysts. **Manufacturing** jobs produce the largest number of **exports** in Singapore. Major exports include electronics and packaged medicine.

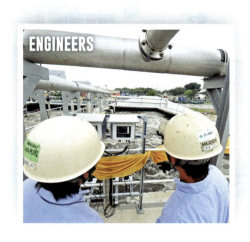

ENGINEERS

MANUFACTURING ELECTRONICS

PLAY

FORMULA 1
SINGAPORE GRAND PRIX

Soccer is the most popular sport in Singapore. Fans support one of eight teams in the professional league. Marina Bay hosts the Formula 1 Singapore Grand Prix race each year. Other sports like badminton and tennis are played year-round.

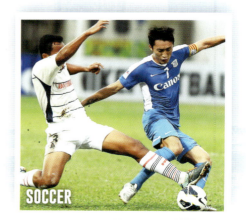

SOCCER

20

Eating out and shopping are enjoyed by many Singaporeans. People also like to gather with neighbors to play games or visit. Many Singaporeans enjoy kayaking, paddle boarding, or scuba diving in the coastal waters. People also enjoy the outdoors by hiking through the many parks, nature reserves, and gardens across the country.

HIKING

SHADOW PUPPETRY

Shadow puppets are flat cutouts with moving pieces that act out plays against a screen.

What You Need:
- construction paper, black or any dark color
- scissors
- glue or tape
- popsicle sticks
- a white bedsheet
- two chairs
- a lamp

What You Do:
1. Start by thinking of a story you want to tell.
2. Draw the shapes of the characters and scenery of your story onto construction paper, and cut them out using scissors.
3. Attach popsicle sticks to your characters with glue or tape. These are your puppets!
4. With tape, attach any scenery pieces to the white bedsheet.
5. Drape the white bedsheet over two chairs placed a few feet apart.
6. Set the lamp behind the bedsheet, and turn it on.
7. Tell your story using your puppets between the lamp and the bedsheet.

FOOD

HAWKER CENTER

Singaporeans eat three meals a day. A popular breakfast is toast with a sweet coconut jam called *kaya* and soft-cooked eggs. Another breakfast favorite is the Indian dish *roti prata*. It is a fluffy pancake with curry.

Hawker centers are groups of food stalls. Many Singaporeans visit these centers for lunch and dinner. Hainanese chicken rice, the unofficial national dish, is a common meal. *Congee* is a rice porridge with meat, seafood, eggs, and peanuts. *Chendol* is a favorite hawker dessert. This iced treat mixes rice flour jelly, coconut milk, and palm sugar.

POPIAH

Ingredients:
- 4 popiah or spring roll wrappers
- 3 tablespoons sweet bean sauce
- 1 tablespoon light soy sauce
- 2 cups shredded jicama
- 1/2 cup bean sprouts
- 1 cup green beans
- 4 to 5 lettuce leaves

Steps:
1. Put one popiah or spring roll wrapper on a plate.
2. Spread as much of each sauce as you like on top of the wrapper.
3. Place a lettuce leaf on top of the sauces, then add as much jicama, bean sprouts, and green beans as you like.
4. Roll the wrapper around the filling snugly.
5. Cut into rounds for easy eating. Enjoy!

CELEBRATIONS

Singapore has many festivals. The Muslim holiday *Hari Raya Puasa* is celebrated at the end of Ramadan. Families gather to eat a feast at sundown. *Deepavali*, the Hindu festival of lights, is celebrated in October or November. Lights fill Little India. Singaporean Christians celebrate Christmas on December 25. Festive lights brighten the streets.

Singaporean families welcome the Chinese New Year in January or February. The festivities last for 15 days. Streets are decorated in red and gold. August 9 is National Day. Singaporeans come together to celebrate the nation's **diverse** population living together!

CHINESE NEW YEAR

GREEN CITY

Tree Planting Day is on the first Sunday of November each year. Singaporeans plant trees around the main island!

DEEPAVALI

TIMELINE

1826
Singapore, along with Malacca and Penang, becomes a colony of the British Empire

14TH CENTURY
Chinese travelers first encounter the original people of Singapore, the seafaring Orang Laut

1965
Singapore becomes an independent nation and joins the United Nations

1922
Singapore becomes the main British naval base in East Asia

1819
The British East India Company establishes their trading post on Singapore island

2008
The first Formula 1 Singapore Grand Prix night race takes place in Marina Bay

1993
Ong Teng Cheong becomes Singapore's first president elected by popular vote

2015
Singapore celebrates 50 years of independence

1988
Dr. Kiat W. Tan sets the vision for the iconic Singapore Botanic Gardens

2017
Halimah Yacob is elected as Singapore's first female president

SINGAPORE FACTS

Official Name: Republic of Singapore

Flag of Singapore: Singapore's flag has two thick horizontal bands. The top band is red. It represents brotherhood and equality. The bottom white band is for purity and virtue. A crescent moon and five stars sit in the left of the red band. The moon symbolizes a young nation, and the five stars represent democracy, peace, progress, justice, and equality.

Area: 278 square miles (719 square kilometers)

Capital City: Singapore

Important Cities: Woodlands, Jurong West, Tampines, Bedok

Population: 5,921,231 (2022 est.)

WHERE PEOPLE LIVE
COUNTRYSIDE 0%
CITY 100%

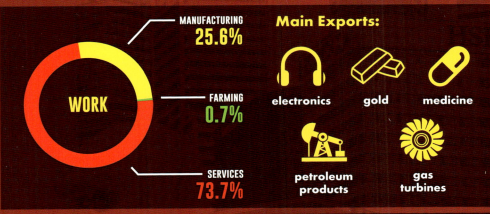

Main Exports: electronics, gold, medicine, petroleum products, gas turbines

WORK: Manufacturing 25.6%, Farming 0.7%, Services 73.7%

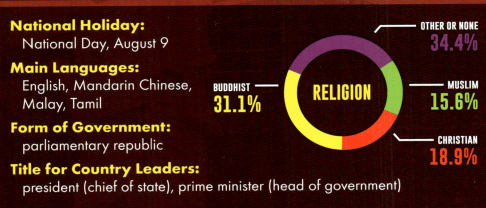

National Holiday:
National Day, August 9

Main Languages:
English, Mandarin Chinese, Malay, Tamil

Form of Government:
parliamentary republic

Title for Country Leaders:
president (chief of state), prime minister (head of government)

RELIGION: Buddhist 31.1%, Other or None 34.4%, Muslim 15.6%, Christian 18.9%

Unit of Money:
Singapore dollar

29

GLOSSARY

city-state—a self-governing city and its surrounding areas

dialects—local ways of speaking particular languages

diverse—made up of people or things that are different from one another

ethnic—related to a group of people who share customs and an identity

exports—products sold by one country to another

face—how someone is seen and judged by others

mangroves—thick tropical forests that can grow along coasts in salty swamp water; mangrove trees have stilt-like roots.

manufacturing—a field of work in which people use machines to make products

monsoon—related to winds that shift direction each season; monsoons bring heavy rain.

mosques—buildings that Muslims use for worship

nature reserves—areas where animals and other natural resources are protected

observatory—a place that provides a wide view

peninsula—a section of land that extends out from a larger piece of land and is almost completely surrounded by water

plateau—an area of flat, raised land

service jobs—jobs that perform tasks for people or businesses

strait—a narrow channel connecting two large bodies of water

urban—related to cities and city life

TO LEARN MORE

AT THE LIBRARY

Kissock, Heather. *Singapore*. New York, N.Y.: AV2, 2022.

Layton, Lesley. *Singapore*. New York, N.Y.: Cavendish Square Publishing, 2022.

Oachs, Emily Rose. *China*. Minneapolis, Minn.: Bellwether Media, 2018.

ON THE WEB

FACTSURFER

Factsurfer.com gives you a safe, fun way to find more information.

1. Go to www.factsurfer.com.

2. Enter "Singapore" into the search box and click 🔍.

3. Select your book cover to see a list of related content.

INDEX

activities, 20, 21
capital (see Singapore)
celebrations, 24-25
Chinese New Year, 24
Christmas, 24
climate, 9
communities, 14-15
customs, 16-17
Deepavali, 24, 25
education, 18
fast facts, 28-29
food, 22-23
Hari Raya Puasa, 24
housing, 14
landmarks, 4, 5
landscape, 5, 8-9, 10
language, 13
location, 6-7
Marina Bay, 5, 8, 20
name, 7
National Day, 24
people, 12-13, 16
Ramadan, 24
recipe, 23
religion, 13, 16, 24

shadow puppetry (activity), 21
Singapore (city), 5, 6, 9, 13, 17
size, 6
sports, 20
Supertree Observatory, 4-5
timeline, 26-27
transportation, 14
Tree Planting Day, 25
wildlife, 10-11
Wong, Fann, 13
work, 19

The images in this book are reproduced through the courtesy of: Vichy Deal, front cover; Perfect Lazybones, pp. 4-5; masion photography, p. 5 (Clarke Quay); Jo Panuwat D, pp. 5 (Cloud Forest), 16; Melinda Nagy, p. 5 (Marina Bay Sands); N_Sakarin, p. 5 (Merlion Park); Aleksandra Tokarz, p. 8; Aerial/ Alamy, p. 9 (top); MEzairi, p. 9 (bottom); Butterfly Hunter, p. 10 (kingfisher); evadeb, p. 10 (hornbill); WildMedia, p. 10 (boar); Christian Musat, p. 10 (otters); Cavan Images/ Alamy, p. 10 (dolphins); Kohyao, pp. 10-11; mentatdgt, p. 12; Adrin Shamsudin, p. 13 (top); Nawadoln, p. 13 (bottom); Travelpixs, p. 14; Jerome Quek, p. 15; chanchai duangdoosan, p. 17; Majority World/ Contributor/ Getty, p. 18; Xinhua/ Alamy, p. 19 (top); Asia File/ Alamy, p. 19 (bottom); Chung Jin Mac/ Alamy, p. 20 (top); South China Morning Post/ Contributor/ Getty, p. 20 (bottom); Nate Hovee, p. 21 (top); WaffelBoo, p. 21 (bottom); EQRoy, p. 22; Chanelio, p. 23 (top); Sarunyu L, p. 23 (middle); perfectloop, p. 23 (bottom); aluxum, p. 24; Buy my stock picture/ Alamy, pp. 24-25; Itar-tass News Agency/ Alamy, p. 27; Glyn Thomas/ Alamy, p. 29 (banknote); money & coins @ ian sanders/ Alamy, p. 29 (coin).